Illustrations by Anna Zakashansky-Zverev

Katya Romanoff

Meeting of the Seasons

Translated from Russian by Svetlana Mitchell

Order this book online at www.trafford.com
or email orders@trafford.com

Most Trafford titles are also available at major online book retailers.

 www.trafford.com

North America & international
toll-free: 844 688 6899 (USA & Canada)
fax: 812 355 4082

Our mission is to efficiently provide the world's finest, most comprehensive book publishing service, enabling every author to experience success. To find out how to publish your book, your way, and have it available worldwide, visit us online at www.trafford.com

Because of the dynamic nature of the Internet, any web addresses or links contained in this book may have changed since publication and may no longer be valid. The views expressed in this work are solely those of the author and do not necessarily reflect the views of the publisher, and the publisher hereby disclaims any responsibility for them.

Illustrations by Anna Zakashansky-Zverev
Translated from Russian by Svetlana Mitchell

ISBN: 978-1-4669-4530-2 *(sc)*
        978-1-4669-4531-9 *(e)*

Library of Congress Control Number: 2012911663

Print information available on the last page.

Trafford rev. 02/28/2021

Illustrations by Anna Zakashansky-Zverev

Katya Romanoff

Meeting of the Seasons

*To all children
who are yet to learn that
Spring always wins*

Translated from Russian by Svetlana Mitchell

Four women met
Once in a thousand years,
Each beautiful and fair,
And prepared to take a stand.

First rose frosty Winter
In her snow-white coat;
She raised her stately brow,
And snow castles appeared.

Hot Summer with rosy cheeks
Melted snow into the lake,
Spread out her green carpet
And then, took a break.

Winter and Summer – powerful beauties:
All that they wished for came true.
And so, as equals, they competed,
And to both shone the Moon.

Between these two queens tossed
The other two – Spring and Autumn.
They'd meet, and then they would scatter,
And soar up above the pine trees.

Autumn, the red-haired diva,
And Spring, freckled and mischievous,
Painted the woods in bright colors
Like two skilful sorceresses.

Autumn scattered leaves without care
And sang in monotonous rain;
While Spring laughed heartily,
And was never the same.

She stormed with thunder and lightning,
And washed the earth clean;
She opened up buds and sprouts
So that her gardens could bloom.

Spring returned birds to the sky,
And caressed all in the sunlight;
Autumn, in turn, was generous
With its harvests and bouquets of fruit.

She gently touched our souls,
Filling them with sweet melancholy.
While Spring embraced so tightly,
And tormented with love – so let it!

In a whirlwind they both swirled
Shooting arrows in gusts of wind,
And awakened passions in people's hearts,
And made the brave rush forward.

Watching all this, Winter and Summer
Went away to their kingdoms,
Leaving Spring and Autumn
To resolve their rivalry on their own.

But Autumn breathed out cold air -
No matter how hard she tried, her time has passed.
Her eyes got dreamy,
And she went out the door.

Spring smiled playfully
And became even more beautiful.
Like a young girl, she shook her curls,
And stood there alone. She won!